Long Ball

The Legend and Lore of the Home Run

MARK STEWART AND MIKE KENNEDY

M Millbrook Press • Minneapolis

Millbrook Press
A division of Lerner Publishing Group
241 First Avenue North
Minneapolis, Minnesota 55401 U.S.A.

Website address: www.lernerbooks.com

Library of Congress Cataloging-in-Publication Data

Stewart, Mark, 1960–
    Long ball : the legend and lore of the home run / by Mark Stewart and Mike Kennedy.
       p. cm.
    Includes bibliographical references and index.
    ISBN-13: 978–0–7613–2779–0 (lib. bdg. : alk. paper)
    ISBN-10: 0–7613–2779–7 (lib. bdg. : alk. paper)
    1. Home runs (Baseball)—United States--History—Juvenile literature. 2. Baseball—Records—
United States—Juvenile literature. 3. Baseball players—Rating of—United States—Juvenile
literature. I. Kennedy, Mike (Mike William), 1965– II. Title.
GV868.4.S74 2006
796.357'26—dc22   2005015041

Manufactured in the United States of America
1 2 3 4 5 6 – DP – 11 10 09 08 07 06

CONTENTS

Introduction

There is no greater thrill in baseball than the simple act of finishing a hit where it started. Whether it happens in the big leagues or in your own backyard makes no difference. Rounding the bases after slugging the ball past the outfielders is a magical feeling that players cherish their entire lives.

This book looks at the "long ball" from many different angles. It explores the history of the home run, and profiles the players who have made it their specialty. You will learn the true stories behind the most famous home runs, and discover the little-known facts about the longest, shortest, and strangest.

The home run represents the pinnacle of personal achievement in American sports. It goes by many names, including *homer*, *four-bagger*, *circuit clout*, *round-tripper*, *moon shot*, *bomb*, *jack*, and, of course, *long ball*. All mean the same thing to a baseball fan: a moment of speed, power, drama, and elation like no other.

The power of the long ball cannot be underestimated. This 12th-inning home run by David Ortiz in Game 4 of the 2004 American League Championship Series ignited an eight-game winning streak that carried the Boston Red Sox from the brink of elimination to their first world championship in 86 years.

1 Touching Them All

THE HISTORY OF THE HOME RUN

When today's baseball fans think of a home run, they picture a long drive off the bat of a hard-swinging slugger that sails over the outfield fence. They imagine the hitter trotting around the bases, touching them all, as the dejected pitcher waits for a fresh ball and a new batter.

In the early days of baseball, this was hardly the case. Yes, a batter managing to propel a pitch out of the park was entitled to circle the bases, but this was an incredibly rare occurrence. Yesterday's home run looked more like today's triple, with the hitter pumping his arms and legs furiously, cutting the bases at full speed, while the fielders set up a frantic relay to head him off.

Baseball has been played in the United States for nearly 200 years, and for all of that time, a home run was the very best hit a batter could make. Yet for at least half of baseball's history, trying to hit the ball over the fence simply was not part of the game. There are many reasons why.

Baseball in the 1880s was not a "power" game. Note the hitter's grip—with his hands spread apart, he was hoping to place the ball between fielders, not slug it over the far-off fences.

Interior Forbes Field, Pittsburgh, Pa.

PHOTO AND COPYRIGHT BY CHAUTAUQUA PHOTOGRAPHING CO., PITTSBURGH, PA.

This postcard of Forbes Field shows how much space there was behind the outfielders in the old ballparks.

Although the old ballparks held far fewer spectators than today's stadiums, they featured huge playing fields with faraway fences. Bats were heavier and had thicker handles than they do today, so it was difficult to produce the swing speed needed to hit a long home run. The balls in use—even at the sport's highest levels—were not well made, and became mushy after being hit a few times. Finally, pitchers did not throw as hard as they do today, so even if a batter swung as hard as he could and hit a pitch perfectly, it might not have enough speed on the way *in* to travel the necessary distance on the way *out*.

With so much going against a batter, why even try to hit a long ball? Well, that was the thinking until the 1920s, when attitudes finally began to change. Before this period, batters swung mostly with their arms and wrists, waiting until the last possible moment to commit themselves. They would literally "aim" the ball between the fielders, and happily take a short single. If a hitter caught a pitch just right, he might line it between the outfielders and, in those old parks, the ball would roll and roll and roll. By the time it was retrieved, a speedy batter might already be halfway to third base, with his coach frantically waving him home. This is how the home run used to look.

On rare occasions, a batter might get lucky and belt one out of the park. This was considered a feat of great strength and skill. Eyewitnesses would talk excitedly about these long balls for days. In 1884, the Chicago Colts (later known as the Cubs) picked up on the growing popularity of over-the-fence home runs. The Colts found themselves competing

The view from Lake Park's oddly angled right-field bleachers. Balls hit into this area were changed from doubles to home runs in 1884.

with two other professional teams for the city's fans that year, so to boost attendance the club changed the ruling on balls popped over the right-field fence in Lake Park, which was less than 250 feet away. Previously, balls that cleared this part of the oddly shaped field were counted as doubles, but for the '84 season, these hits would count as home runs. Chicago hit 142 homers that year—131 at Lake Park and only 11 on the road. The Colts' third baseman, Ned Williamson, slugged 27 home runs to set a new record. Williamson's mark would stand for 35 seasons, because in 1885 the Colts moved to a new park and the league passed a rule outlawing "cheap" home runs.

Baseball remained a game of short hits, daring baserunning, tricky pitching, and great strategy until a raw-boned teenager named George

Babe Ruth warms up for the Boston Red Sox. He was the top left-handed pitcher in baseball before he became famous for his home runs.

Ruth came along. Ruth was a fabulous pitcher and a fearsome slugger—probably the best natural athlete the game had ever seen. What made him truly different, however, was that he had not learned the "right" way to play baseball. The man nicknamed "Babe" played the game the "fun" way, and that meant swinging as hard as he could at every pitch, and trying to hit the ball as far as he could. And oh, could he hit the long ball. In an era when a 300-foot line drive was considered a "muscle shot," Ruth hit towering fly balls that regularly traveled more than 400 feet.

People who had never seen Ruth were amazed when they watched him step to the plate. Whereas his teammates and opponents were stabbing and chopping at pitches to avoid the embarrassment of missing the ball completely, Ruth often swung so hard he fell down! This amused some and disgusted others. Where did this big dope come from, they wondered, and where on earth did he learn to play baseball? The answer was that Ruth had learned the game in reform school; he had never received any kind of coaching. He played ball the only way he knew how, like an overgrown kid.

Ruth was a full-time pitcher and part-time outfielder until the 1919 season, when the Boston Red Sox made him a full-time outfielder and part-time pitcher. It was not an easy choice, because he happened to be the best left-handed pitcher in the league. In that first season as an everyday player, Ruth slugged 29 home runs to set a new record. Fans who had once jeered him now cheered him— even when he struck out. America had just gone through a horrible war and a deadly influenza epidemic, and people seemed to appreciate a player who wasn't afraid to risk making a fool of himself to entertain them with a long ball.

The Red Sox sold Ruth to the New York Yankees prior to the 1920 season. Encouraged to swing hard and often, he obliterated his own record with 54 home runs. In that remarkable year, Ruth out-homered every other team in the league, and the runner-up to Ruth, George Sisler, managed just 19 round-trippers. Ruth's popularity went through the roof, and the long ball became the talk of the sports

Babe Ruth follows through on one of his big swings. Ruth's long balls changed the way baseball was played.

TY COBB

Ty Cobb prided himself on his "scientific" hitting. He did not like the way baseball changed.

world. His home runs made headlines in every newspaper in America, from the largest cities to the smallest towns.

Not everyone was swept up in the long ball frenzy of the 1920s. Ty Cobb (baseball's greatest player at the time) despised the home run for taking the strategy out of the game. He hated Ruth, and never forgave him for "ruining" baseball. Other players, especially those looking to make a name for themselves, were quick to copy Ruth's slugging style. They adjusted their swings and started aiming for the fences, and soon the long ball became baseball's biggest drawing card. The more often fly balls sailed over outfield fences, the more attendance soared.

Baseball encouraged power hitting by outlawing pitches like the spitball, and by making sure bright new balls were always in play. Home runs also increased when, starting in 1931, hits down the foul lines were judged by where they passed the foul pole, instead of where they landed.

Ever since the Babe came on the scene, power hitters have ruled the game. Pitching and defense are still needed to win championships, but home runs are what the fans come to see. As Cobb had feared, the long ball did indeed eliminate some of the sport's traditional strategies. Yet it also created many *new* strategies, along with millions of new fans who were attracted by the drama and excitement of the home run. Teams that had power hitters built their lineups around the long ball, while teams that did not still "manufactured" runs the old-fashioned way. Baseball changed, but at its heart the game remained the same.

2 Forever Famous

TEN GREAT LONG BALLS

Want to start an argument among baseball experts? Just ask who hit history's greatest long ball. There have been hundreds of dramatic home runs over the years, and every fan has his or her favorite. Choosing one as the absolute all-time best is impossible.

The details of a legendary home run are like the ingredients in a gourmet meal. To be considered one of the best ever, a long ball has to be created by a well known player. If it does not change the course of a season or championship, it must, at the very least, rewrite the history books or add to the legend and lore of baseball. Also, a great long ball must be struck at a moment when the crowd is brimming with anticipation, so that the sight of the ball flying out of the park brings the fans leaping to their feet.

Who hit history's most memorable long ball? The following pages look at 10 of the best... read on and join the debate!

"The Babe Calls His Shot"
October 1, 1932 • Wrigley Field, Chicago

After watching the Philadelphia A's beat them out of the American League pennant three years in a row, the New York Yankees found the right mix of young players and old stars in 1932 and made it back to the World Series. No one was happier than Babe Ruth, who was beginning to slow down at age 37 and feared he might never again play on the big stage. The Yankees faced the NL champion Chicago Cubs, and demolished them in the first two games at Yankee Stadium.

The Cubs' fans were angry and frustrated by the time the teams met for Game 3 in Wrigley Field, and Ruth was the main target for their insults. The Chicago players joined in, hoping to distract the Babe,

Babe Ruth watches the ball disappear into the bleachers as he starts his home run trot. The "Bambino" could change a game with one swing, as he did against the Cubs in 1932.

but it did not work—he loved the attention! In the fifth inning, with the score tied 4–4, pitcher Charlie Root burned a called strike past Ruth, and the jeering got louder. Ruth held up one finger to remind the Cubs that it was just one strike. Root's second pitch was a strike, too, and Ruth held up a second finger.

With everyone in the ballpark screaming at the Babe, he then pointed toward center field and yelled something to the players in the Cubs' dugout. It was so noisy, no one really heard what he said. To Cubs' fans, it looked as if he was boldly predicting a home run, and they booed even louder. Root challenged the slugger with his next delivery, and Ruth pounded it far over the center-field wall for a home run. Did Ruth "call" his shot? No one knows for sure. Moments later, Lou Gehrig drove a ball over the fence and the Cubs were dead. They lost the game 7–5, and fell the next day 13–6 for a humiliating four-game sweep.

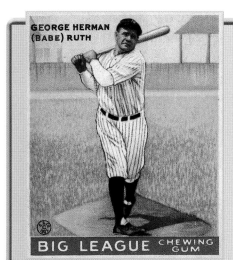

GEORGE HERMAN (BABE) RUTH

BIG LEAGUE CHEWING GUM

Collector's Corner

The Hitter
BABE RUTH

This was Ruth's final World Series appearance. Though slowed down by his weight, he was still a dangerous hitter. Ruth batted .341 with 41 home runs in 1932.

1933 Goudey Gum
Babe Ruth Card

The Pitcher
CHARLIE ROOT

Root, a 33-year-old veteran with a mean streak, insisted that Ruth did not "call" his shot. He claimed he would have thrown the next pitch at Ruth's head if he thought the Yankee star was predicting a home run.

1939 Goudey Gum
"Charley" Root Premium Photo

Baseball card and memorabilia collectors love the challenge of collecting by "subject." The sidebars pages 15-33 highlight collectibles of the hitters and pitchers who were part of history's most famous home runs.

"Thomson Hits Shot Heard 'Round the World"

OCTOBER 3, 1951 • POLO GROUNDS, NEW YORK CITY

Only once in the history of baseball has a league championship been ripped from the grasp of one team and delivered to another with a home run in the bottom of the ninth inning. This occurred at the conclusion of the 1951 season, after the New York Giants staged a historic comeback to tie the Brooklyn Dodgers for first place in the National League pennant race. A best-of-three playoff was held to determine the title, and the bitter rivals split the first two games.

Bobby Thomson follows the flight of his pennant-winning home run.

The Dodgers had their ace, Don Newcombe, on the mound for Game 3. He held the Giants to one run through eight innings, while Brooklyn scored four times to take a commanding lead. In the bottom of the ninth, Newcombe ran out of gas, allowing one more run to cross the plate. He left the game with the score 4–2, one out, and two runners on base. Manager Chuck Dressen had to decide between Carl Erskine, a curveball specialist, and Ralph Branca, a 21-year-old with a blazing fastball. Dressen chose Branca, despite the fact that the next batter, Bobby Thomson, had already homered against him earlier in the series.

Thomson watched Branca's first pitch sail by for a called strike. Vowing not to let another good one go, he jumped on the next delivery even though it was high and inside. Thomson drove the ball on a line to left field. Thinking it would hit the wall, he broke from the batter's box hoping for a double. When he saw the ball disappear into the stands, he rounded the bases in jubilation. The Giants won the game 5–4, and with it the NL pennant.

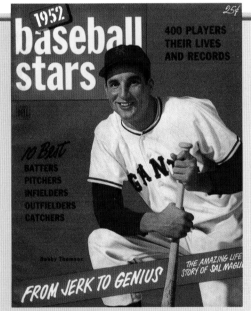

1952 Bobby Thomson
Baseball Stars Magazine

The Hitter
BOBBY THOMSON

Thomson was an All-Star in 1948, '49, and '52 for the Giants, and hit 24 or more home runs six times in seven full seasons with the team. He was traded to the Braves in 1954 and broke his ankle in spring training. This opened the way for a 20-year-old named Hank Aaron to win a starting job.

The Pitcher
RALPH BRANCA

Branca came up to the Dodgers as a teenager during World War II. He won 21 games for Brooklyn at the age of 21 in 1947. Branca hurt his arm in 1952 and never pitched well again. He and Thomson became good friends and made hundreds of public appearances together.

1953 Bowman Ralph Branca Card

"Maz Sinks Yankee Battleship"

OCTOBER 13, 1960 • FORBES FIELD, PITTSBURGH

The 1960 World Series was one of the strangest ever. The New York Yankees, starring Mickey Mantle and Roger Maris, outscored the Pittsburgh Pirates 46–15 in the first six games—yet the series was tied at three games each. Game 7 was a crazy seesaw battle, with Pittsburgh taking a 4–0 lead and the Yankees coming back to score seven runs. The Pirates staged a dramatic five-run rally in the eighth inning to assume command at 9–7, but New York tied the score 9–9 in the top of the ninth.

Ralph Terry, who had been brought in by the Yankees to get the final out

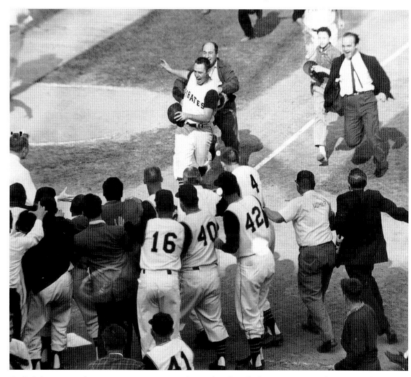

Bill Mazeroski is just a step ahead of jubilant Pirate fans as he meets his teammates at home plate. "Maz" was known more for his glove than his bat, but he was one of the best hitters at his position when he played.

of the eighth inning, took the mound for New York in the bottom of the ninth. He was due to face Pittsburgh's number-eight hitter, Bill Mazeroski, a pinch hitter for the pitcher, and then the top of the order. Terry threw a high fastball to the Pirates' second baseman, who let it go.

Expecting another fastball, Mazeroski turned on Terry's next pitch and drove it over the left-field wall to end the game. Forbes Field erupted in wild celebration as Mazeroski circled the bases. He had hit what is still the one and only Game 7 "walk-off" home run in World Series history.

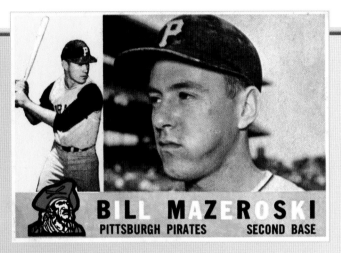

The Hitter
BILL MAZEROSKI

Mazeroski was the finest defensive second baseman in history, and not a bad hitter. His 11 home runs in 1960 were the most among all second basemen. "Maz" was elected to the Hall of Fame in 2001.

1960 Topps Bill Mazeroski Card

The Pitcher
RALPH TERRY

Terry had little trouble with Mazeroski when he had faced him in Game 4. He struck out Mazeroski and also retired him on a pop-up. Terry recovered from his Game 7 defeat to pitch well for the Yankees, winning 56 games over the next three seasons.

1960 Topps Ralph Terry Card

"Roger Maris Blasts #61"
OCTOBER 1, 1961 • YANKEE STADIUM, THE BRONX

During the 1930s, '40s, and '50s, many sluggers had tried to beat Babe Ruth's record of 60 home runs in a season, but all had failed. In 1961, Mickey Mantle and Roger Maris launched an assault on that magic number. All summer long, the two Yankee teammates (they were also friends and roommates) matched each other, long ball for long ball. Mantle was the guy the fans were rooting for, but when a leg injury cut short his season after 54 home runs, Maris had to continue alone.

Maris was a quiet man who did not seek fame or attention. In fact, he was unknown to most Americans before coming to the Yankees in 1960. Now, like it or not, he was the most-watched athlete in the country. As Maris closed in on Ruth, the pressure reached a fever pitch. He was so nervous his hair started to fall out. Maris hit number 60 with nearly a week to go in the season, but could not get number 61.

Roger Maris completes his record-breaking swing, homering to right field against the Red Sox on the final day of the 1961 season.

In the final game of the year, the Yankees faced the Red Sox. Tracy Stallard was on the mound for Boston. He retired Maris on a fly ball in the first inning. In the fourth, Maris worked the count to two balls and no strikes. He knew Stallard's next pitch would be right over the plate. Maris got good wood on the ball and sent it screaming into the right-field seats. The crowd exploded as he circled the bases wearing one of the biggest smiles in baseball history.

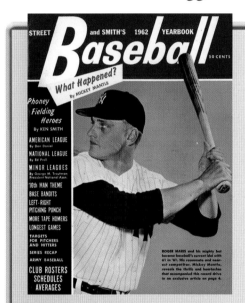

The Hitter
ROGER MARIS

Maris was an excellent all-around player who had a perfect swing for Yankee Stadium's short right-field fence. Because the season was expanded from 154 games to 162 games in 1961, commissioner Ford Frick (a friend of Ruth's), considered making Maris's record separate from the Babe's. Maris played on seven pennant winners during the 1960s, more than anyone else in baseball.

1962 Roger Maris *Street & Smith's* Magazine

The Pitcher
TRACY STALLARD

Stallard was a 6' 5" rookie making his fourteenth start of the season. He suffered two other unlucky defeats in his career, both in 1964. Stallard was the losing pitcher in history's longest game (7 hours, 23 minutes) and was facing Jim Bunning when the Hall of Famer threw a perfect game on Father's Day.

1961 Topps Tracy Stallard Card

"Hammerin' Hank Passes the Babe"
April 8, 1974 • Fulton County Stadium, Atlanta

Hank Aaron hit 40 home runs during the 1973 season, leaving him with a career total of 713, one short of Babe Ruth's all-time record. All winter long, the excitement, anticipation, and pressure built up for numbers 714 and 715. When would Aaron hit them? Where would he hit them? Which pitcher would go down in history as the man who served up the record-breaker? By the time the 1974 season began, Aaron was exhausted from all of the questions and just wanted to get it over and done with.

Everyone follows the flight of Hank Aaron's historic home run as it soars toward left field.

Number 714 came in the season opener against the Cincinnati Reds. Now it was just a matter of time before Aaron would break the Babe's record. But how much time? The longer it took, the more the pressure would mount. Aaron dreaded the thought of a long wait for number 715, so in the next game he played, against the Dodgers, he was looking for just the right pitch.

Pitcher Al Downing had been around for more than 10 years, and he was not about to make it easy for Aaron. In the first inning, the left-hander tried to get him to swing at bad pitches, but Aaron resisted the temptation and drew a walk. In the fourth inning, with a runner on first, Aaron knew Downing would try to throw a slider and make him hit into a double play. Sure enough, he got the ball he was expecting on the second pitch, and pulled it into the left-field bullpen. Just two hits into the young season, Aaron was crowned baseball's new home run champion.

Baseball

Henry Aaron

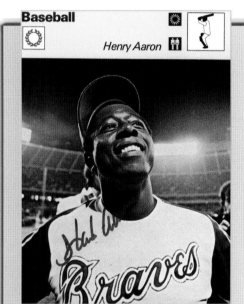

The Hitter
HANK AARON

Aaron received death threats all winter from racist fans who did not want an African-American to surpass Babe Ruth. He finished the 1974 season with 20 home runs. Aaron played his final two years with the Milwaukee Brewers, ending his career in the same city where he had started, with a total of 755 long balls.

1978 Hank Aaron Sportscaster Card

The Pitcher
AL DOWNING

In 1961, Downing became the first African-American pitcher to start a game for the New York Yankees. By 1974, he had lost his good fastball, but he had learned to pitch well enough to win 20 games.

1963 Al Downing *Baseball Digest* Magazine

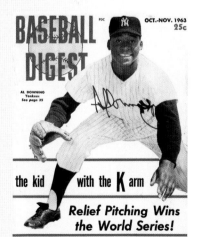

BASEBALL DIGEST

OCT.–NOV. 1963
25c

AL DOWNING
Yankees
See page 35

the kid with the K arm

Relief Pitching Wins the World Series!

Are Mets Bad for Baseball?

23

"Pudge Puts the Reds to Bed"
OCTOBER 22, 1975 • FENWAY PARK, BOSTON

The 1975 World Series already was one of the best ever when Game 6 started in Boston on a chilly October evening. The Reds had won three times and the Red Sox twice, but Boston fans were confident about their team's chances. Their hearts sank, however, when Cincinnati drove their ace, Luis Tiant, from the mound in the eighth inning. Boston was able to tie the game in the bottom of the inning and nearly won it in the

Carlton Fisk leaps high in the air after his home run clears the Green Monster in Fenway Park. Game 6 of the 1975 World Series began on October 21st and ended at 12:01 A.M. on October 22nd.

ninth. Fans in New England held their breath as this thrilling game went into extra innings, tied 6–6.

The Red Sox thwarted a Cincinnati rally in the tenth inning. Right fielder Dwight Evans prevented a Cincinnati home run with a great catch in the eleventh. Two Reds runners were stranded on base in the twelfth. Fenway Park was going wild—and millions of fans were riveted to their televisions—when Carlton Fisk led off the bottom of the twelfth at the stroke of midnight. He belted Pat Darcy's second pitch high and deep down the left-field line.

The TV camera followed Fisk as he used all of his powers to "keep" the ball fair. He hopped up and down, yelled at the ball, and tried to wave it away from foul territory. When the ball clanked off the foul pole, Fisk leaped into the air and circled the bases in celebration. Never before had the drama and emotion of baseball been captured so perfectly on the small screen. It was a breathtaking moment for the game.

Collector's Corner

The Hitter
CARLTON FISK

Fisk was one of the most durable catchers in history, but he had missed half the team's games in 1975 with a broken arm and he hit only 10 home runs. He played 23 seasons, hit 376 home runs, and was elected to the Hall of Fame in 2000.

1975 SSPC Carlton Fisk Card

The Pitcher
Pat Darcy

Darcy battled injuries his entire career, but had a good year in 1975 with 11 wins. The Reds won Game 7 by a score of 4–3 the next night, but Fisk's long ball is the moment everyone remembers from the '75 World Series.

1975 SSPC Pat Darcy Card

"Mr. October Destroys the Dodgers"

OCTOBER 18, 1977 • YANKEE STADIUM, THE BRONX

The New York Yankees returned to the World Series for the first time in a dozen seasons in 1976, only to be humiliated by the Cincinnati Reds in a four-game sweep. That winter, owner George Steinbrenner opened his wallet and hired Reggie Jackson, baseball's most dynamic player. Jackson had a big personality that did not fit in well with the no-nonsense Yankees, but he also had three championship rings, which were won as a member of the Oakland A's. Jackson was

Reggie Jackson whips his bat through the hitting zone as he launches a long ball in Game 6 of the 1977 World Series.

nicknamed "Mr. October" because he was at his best in the World Series. So when New York won the pennant again in 1977, all eyes were on Reggie as the Yankees faced the Dodgers for the championship.

New York won three of the first four games, but Los Angeles beat the Yankees badly in Game 5 and looked like they were on a roll. The pressure was really on the Yankees in Game 6—if they lost, the Dodgers would be tough to beat in Game 7. When Los Angeles took a 3–2 lead in the third inning, the fans began to worry. They needed a hero.

Jackson stepped in against Burt Hooton in the fourth inning with a man on first base and hit a long home run to give New York a 4–3 lead. In the fifth inning, he made the score 7–3 when he lined a pitch by Elias Sosa into the right-field seats. With two homers on two swings, Jackson had turned the game around. Now it was time to have fun. When he came up in the eighth inning, Charlie Hough threw him a knuckleball and he crushed it into the center-field bleachers for one of the longest long balls in Yankee Stadium history. Jackson's feat of three home runs on three swings has never been matched in World Series play.

REGGIE JACKSON
New York YANKEES
OUTFIELD

The Hitter
REGGIE JACKSON

Jackson also hit home runs in Game 4 and Game 5, giving him a record five for the World Series. His career batting average in World Series play was .357 and he slammed a total of 10 long balls in 27 games.

1977 Hostess Reggie Jackson Card

The Pitchers
BURT HOOTON, ELIAS SOSA, AND CHARLIE HOUGH

Hooton and Hough were good pitchers who won a combined 367 games in their careers. Sosa was cut by the Dodgers after the 1977 World Series, but pitched well for the Montreal Expos in 1979 and '80.

1978 Topps Charlie Hough Card

CHARLIE HOUGH

"Bucky's Blast Beats Boston"

OCTOBER 2, 1978 • FENWAY PARK, BOSTON

Bucky Dent gets the head of his bat on a slider by Mike Torrez and drives it toward Fenway Park's left-field wall. His home run put the Yankees ahead 3–2 in their playoff with the Red Sox.

After falling 14 games behind the Boston Red Sox in the summer of 1978, the New York Yankees went on an amazing run to finish with 99 wins. The Red Sox also won 99, meaning the AL East would be decided in a one-game playoff. Ron Guidry took the mound for the Yankees and threw a great game, but Boston's Mike Torrez, an ex-Yankee, pitched even better. Boston led 2–0 after six innings.

Torrez got into a jam in the seventh, allowing two base runners. With two outs, he went right after New York's ninth-place hitter, Bucky Dent. Torrez delivered a late-breaking slider, which Dent fouled off his foot. He fell to the ground in agony, and promised himself that he would be ready if Torrez tried the same pitch again.

Sure enough, the big righty delivered another slider to the same spot. Dent got the head of his bat on the ball, and lifted a high fly down the left-field line. The ball settled into the screen near the foul pole atop Fenway's famous "Green Monster" for a three-run homer and a 3–2 lead. The Yankees scored twice more and held on to win the game, 5–4.

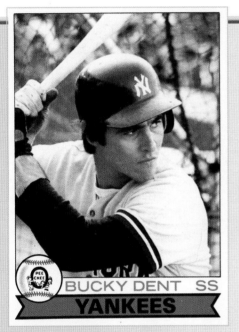

Collector's Corner

The Hitter
BUCKY DENT

Dent was a sure-handed All-Star shortstop, but a streaky hitter. He went on to bat .417 with 7 RBIs in the 1978 World Series against the Dodgers. He now owns a baseball school in Florida that features a miniature version of Boston's "Green Monster."

1979 O-Pee-Chee Bucky Dent Card

The Pitcher
MIKE TORREZ

Torrez won the final game of the 1977 World Series for the Yankees, and then signed with the rival Red Sox as a free agent for 1978. He was one of the most consistent winners of the 1970s.

1978 Topps Mike Torrez Card

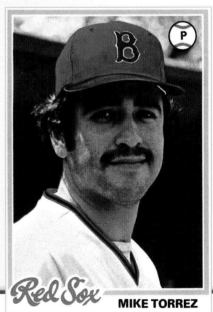

"Gimpy Gibson Guts the A's"

OCTOBER 15, 1988 • DODGER STADIUM, LOS ANGELES

Kirk Gibson was the heart and soul of the Los Angeles Dodgers in 1988, inspiring a so-so team to the NL pennant, and winning the Most Valuable Player award for his leadership. When he injured his leg in the final game of the playoffs, however, his teammates doubted they had a chance against the powerful Oakland A's in the World Series. Prior to Game 1, the Dodger star was sitting in the clubhouse watching the pregame show on television. Announcer Bob Costas kept repeating the fact that Gibson was too hurt to play, making him angrier and angrier.

When the game started, Gibson told manager Tommy Lasorda that, if he needed it, he had one big swing to offer before his body gave out. The Dodgers went into the bottom of the ninth trailing 4–3. On the mound for the A's was the great Dennis Eckersley. He retired the first two hitters, but walked Mike Davis. Lasorda told Gibson to grab a bat.

Eckersley went right at Gibson with two wicked fastballs. Gibson grimaced in pain as he defended the plate and fouled each away. The Oakland reliever could not get the Dodger star

Kirk Gibson pumps his fist in triumph after his dramatic World Series home run off of Dennis Eckersley.

to nibble at three bad pitches, and the count was full. Gibson recalled that Eckersley sometimes used a sneaky "back-door" slider in this situation and decided to look for the pitch. When he saw it coming he unleashed the greatest swing he could muster and pounded the ball into the right-field bleachers to win the game. Gibson could barely limp around the bases. Lasorda could not contain his tears. Gibson did not play another inning in the World Series, but he had done all he needed to—the Dodgers defeated the shell-shocked A's, 4 games to 1.

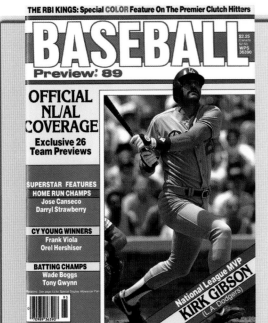

Collector's Corner

The Hitter
KIRK GIBSON

Gibson was an All-American football star in college and one of baseball's best all-around athletes. He led the Detroit Tigers to the championship in 1984, and signed with the Dodgers as a free agent before the 1988 season.

1989 Kirk Gibson
Baseball Preview Magazine

The Pitcher
DENNIS ECKERSLEY

A 20-game winner as a starting pitcher, Eckersley was even better as a reliever. In 1988, he saved 45 games to lead the major leagues. Eckersley was voted into the Hall of Fame in 2004.

1994 Score Dennis Eckersley Card

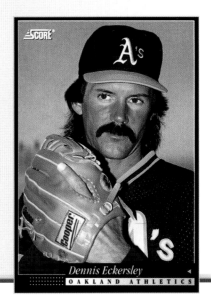

Dennis Eckersley
OAKLAND ATHLETICS

"Big Mac Mashes #62"

September 8, 1998 • Busch Memorial Stadium, St. Louis

After a fight between the owners and players led to the cancellation of the 1994 World Series, baseball was a wounded game. Millions of fans stopped caring, and it seemed as if nothing could draw them back. Finally, two very special players— Mark McGwire and Sammy Sosa— were able to win their hearts. The two power hitters dueled all year long for the long ball lead, inching closer and closer to Roger Maris's record of 61 home runs.

Early in September, the St. Louis Cardinals hosted the Chicago Cubs. McGwire hit number 61 to tie Maris in the opening game of the series, belting a towering home run off the window of the faraway Stadium Club. The next night, McGwire faced Steve Trachsel, who was known for keeping the ball low. Sure enough, the Chicago righty delivered a sinking fastball. McGwire reached down and golfed a line drive down the left-field line. It looked like a double at first, but it had just

Mark McGwire drills a pitch by Steve Trachsel down the left-field line for his record-setting 62nd home run of the 1998 season.

enough carry to sneak over the fence. McGwire's shortest long ball of the year turned out to be his biggest!

After circling the bases, the St. Louis slugger was greeted by his son, Matthew. McGwire lifted him high in the air in celebration. Sosa trotted in from right field to give McGwire a hug. The new home run champion also received congratulations from the Maris family. It was a heartwarming ending to a thrilling race. Baseball was finally *back*.

Collector's Corner

The Hitter
MARK MCGWIRE

After falling behind Sosa later in September, McGwire finished 1998 with a bang, hitting five homers in his last three games to end up with 70.

1998 Mark McGwire *Sports Illustrated* Magazine

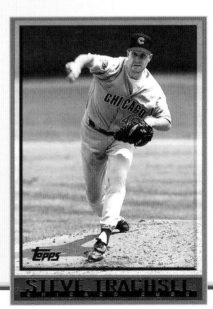

The Pitcher
STEVE TRACHSEL

Trachsel's 15 victories in 1998 helped the Cubs make the playoffs as the NL Wild Card team. He gave up 27 long balls during the season, but only 6 with runners on base.

1998 Topps Steve Trachsel Card

3 Long Ball Legends

THE ART OF HITTING HOME RUNS

here is no special trick to hitting a long ball. Just about anyone who is good enough to play in the major leagues is capable of doing it. When a professional hitter meets a pitch with the "sweet spot" of his bat, and gets under it just a bit, the ball has an excellent chance of clearing the outfield wall.

That is *not* to say hitting home runs is easy. It takes a near-perfect swing to send a darting, spinning, 90-mph pitch into the seats. Indeed, most hitters will tell you that the harder they try to hit a long ball, the more difficult it is to do so.

Over the years, a select group of players has made the long ball something of a specialty. Each did it a little bit differently from those who came before and after him, and each added a creative flair or some other personal touch to the strong body and sharp eye all hitters need. Among their peers, these individuals are more than mere "stars." They are considered *artists* of the long ball.

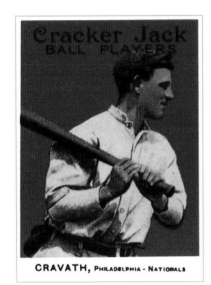

CRAVATH, Philadelphia - Nationals

GAVY CRAVATH   1908–1919

The Baker Bowl in Philadelphia, home of the Phillies from 1895 to 1938, may have been the best hitter's park in history. It had very cozy outfield dimensions, including a wall in right–center field that was less than 300 feet from home plate. Obviously, every batter took aim at this tasty target, but only one, right-handed Gavy Cravath, perfected the art of lining hits over that fence. In 1914, he led the National League with 19 home runs, and *all* of them came at the Baker Bowl! Cravath was history's first long ball "specialist"—he led the NL six times between 1913 and 1919—and he is still the only home run champion whose best hits went to the opposite field.

BABE RUTH   1914–1935

Babe Ruth established the art of modern power hitting. His goal every time he came to the plate was to hit the ball as hard and as far as he possibly could. Unlike the top batters of his era, whose goal was to simply make solid contact and place their hits between fielders, Ruth attacked the ball with his entire body. Instead of keeping his feet planted in the batter's box, he took a big stride as the pitcher hurled the ball toward him, moving the weight of his body forward while still keeping his hips, upper body, and arms coiled behind him. As Ruth dug his front foot into the dirt, he turned his hips quickly and began to whip his big, heavy bat into motion above his back shoulder. Next, as he deter-

BABE RUTH

mined the speed, spin, and location of the pitch, he brought his arms through the hitting zone, rotated his shoulders, and snapped his wrists at the instant his bat met the ball. Ruth usually added an uppercut to his swing, so when he hit a pitch out in front of him and caught it just below center, the ball had a lot of backspin and soared in a long, majestic arc. He led the league in home runs 12 times between 1918 and 1931, and finished with 714 in his career.

LOU GEHRIG   1923–1939

Lou Gehrig was a savage hitter whose compact swing produced sizzling grounders and screaming line drives. After two years as Babe Ruth's teammate, he learned how to loft pitches into the bleachers, and became a formidable long ball hitter. In 1927, when Ruth set a new record with 60 home runs, Gehrig matched him homer-for-homer for most of the summer, but fell short at 47. Opponents faced a terrible dilemma when they played the Yankees: Do you risk throwing strikes to Ruth, the third hitter in the lineup, or do you "pitch around" him to face Gehrig, the fourth hitter, who was younger, stronger, and harder to strike out?

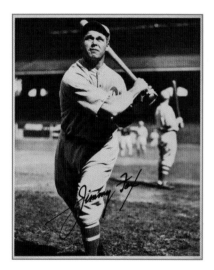

JIMMIE FOXX   1925–1945

Jimmie Foxx might have been the strongest long ball hitter in history. In an era when baseball players did not believe in lifting weights or overdeveloping their bodies, he was so muscular that he was nicknamed the "Beast." Foxx's swing was like an explosion. He was one of the young hitters who modeled himself after Babe Ruth, and by the late 1920s he had matched the Babe for sheer power. In 1932, Foxx hit 58 home runs, and "lost" five homers to a screen at Sportsman's Park in St. Louis that had *not* been there when Ruth hit 60 in 1927.

JOSH GIBSON   1930–1946

The unwritten rule that banned African-American players from the major leagues until after World War II robbed the game of its greatest power-hitting catcher. A star in the Negro Leagues, Josh Gibson was a big man with big dreams, and a big talent for hitting the long ball. He was so strong and so quick that he did not have to stride into pitches. He kept both feet planted in the batter's box and started his swing by swiveling his hips toward the pitcher as the ball approached the plate, then whipping his bat through the hitting zone. The major leaguers who played against Gibson in exhibition games during the 1930s swore he was every bit as powerful as Babe Ruth, Lou Gehrig, and Jimmie Foxx. Among the many long balls Gibson swatted were two home runs at Yankee Stadium that each traveled more than 550 feet. He died of a stroke at age 35, brokenhearted that he never got to prove himself in the big leagues.

TED WILLIAMS   1939–1960

Ted Williams had a long, smooth swing that is still regarded as the most beautiful the game has ever known. He was a student of hitting, regarding it more as a science than an art. Unable to "muscle" balls over the fences like traditional power hitters, the stick-thin Williams recognized that his type of swing would still produce long balls, but only off certain pitches in certain locations. Williams analyzed every type of pitch in every part of the strike zone, and found that a pitcher had the advantage on many, while the batter had the advantage on only a few. Most times, he simply refused to offer at a pitch that was not to his liking. The result was a .344 lifetime average, 2,019 walks, and 521 home runs.

RALPH KINER   1946–1955

Ralph Kiner of the Pittsburgh Pirates led the National League in home runs the first seven years of his career—a feat that has never been equaled. He hit home runs by waiting for balls on the inside half of the plate, and then pulling them into the stands. Kiner did not see many good pitches, because he was surrounded by poor hitters in the lineup. Most of his long balls came on pitchers' "mistakes." The one advantage Kiner *did* have was a fenced-in bullpen area in his home park, which reduced the distance to the left-field power alley from 406 to 355 feet, turning long fly balls into home runs. This became his specialty, and the bullpen came to be called "Kiner's Korner."

MICKEY MANTLE   1951–1968

The term "tape-measure home run" came into fashion during the reign of Mickey Mantle. A switch-hitter, he possessed awesome strength that enabled him to hit historic homers from both sides of the plate. Outside of Babe Ruth, no long ball specialist swung as hard or produced drives as great as Mantle. He first raised eyebrows as a rookie during spring training in 1951, when he hit a ball out of the University of Southern California's Bovard Stadium— and across the *football field* behind it! Like Ruth, when Mantle saw a pitch he liked, he took an "all-or-nothing" swing that had an electric effect on the crowd. Fans never left the stadium—no matter how lopsided the score—if Mantle was due to bat one more time.

WILLIE MAYS   1951–1973

Only a handful of players can say they did "everything" well in baseball—run, throw, field, hit for average, and hit for power. Of that small group, Willie Mays was the best at hitting the long ball. He threw his whole body into every sweeping swing, generating force so great that it twisted him backward as he followed through. Mays's grounders cut quickly through the infield, his line drives seemed to hang in the air an extra second or two, and the fly balls he belted had that extra few feet they needed to reach the seats. Mays topped 50 home runs twice (10 years apart!) and did so playing in parks that were not kind to right-handed gap hitters (the Polo Grounds and Candlestick Park). The most remarkable thing about the "Amazing Mays" was that he was as good a center fielder and base runner as he was a hitter—some say the best all-around star the game has ever known.

Made for Television

In 1959, American Motors turned the long ball into "reality TV" when the company sponsored *Home Run Derby*. The show featured two of baseball's top sluggers each week in a one-on-one power-hitting duel. Sportscaster Mark Scott would interview one player while the other one hit, and the stars would often compare their techniques.

HANK AARON
MILWAUKEE BRAVES

HANK AARON   1954–1976

Hank Aaron was the best "wrist-hitter" of the modern era. His wrists were so quick and strong that he could wait an additional fraction of a second before deciding where to aim the barrel of his bat. That extra time enabled Aaron to hit balls so hard and so squarely that they made a distinctly different sound when they came off his bat—like a rifle shot, some said. During his 12 years in Milwaukee's spacious County Stadium, no one thought of Aaron as a long ball hitter, though he did lead the National League twice. When the Braves moved to Atlanta in 1966, however, Aaron saw how short it was down the left-field line, and adjusted his swing to take advantage of the new dimensions. His quick wrists produced 315 home runs between the ages of 32 and 39, which are often a hitter's "declining" years. This put Aaron within reach of Babe Ruth's all-time record of 714, which he surpassed early in the 1974 season to become the sport's new home run king.

HARMON KILLEBREW   1954–1975

Harmon Killebrew was a muscular slugger whose batting style demanded perfect timing and great strength. He started his swing with the barrel of his bat tilted toward the pitcher and then ripped it across the plate at a tremendous speed. For the first five years of his career (he made it to the majors at age 17), this approach created a lot more pop-ups and strikeouts than long balls. In 1958, Killebrew had a grand total of *zero* home runs. A year later, he found his groove and blasted 42—and ended up surpassing the 40 mark eight times between 1959 and 1970. Killebrew would wait patiently all day for that one pitch he could drive, making him a pitcher's nightmare. The fact that his lifetime batting average was only .256 just goes to show how misleading a statistic this can be.

FRANK ROBINSON   1956–1976

In the war between batter and pitcher, each usually concedes a little territory to the other. The batter claims the inside part of the strike zone, while the outer edge of the strike zone belongs to the pitcher. Frank Robinson wanted the whole strike zone for himself. He took his position at the inner edge of the right-hand batter's box, with his knees and elbows mere inches from the black outline of home plate. He strode confidently into every pitch, crushing balls on the inside half to left field, and driving balls on the outside half to right field. Although he finished his career with 583 home runs, Robinson paid a price for his stubborness. Pitchers hated him, and sent him sprawling to the ground with "bean balls" (pitches aimed at the head) in almost every game he played. Of course, this made him even more determined to hold his ground. Many times, Robinson dusted himself off, stepped back into the box, and hit one right back at the mound—or completely out of the park.

REGGIE JACKSON   1967–1987

With the possible exception of Babe Ruth, no one enjoyed hitting the long ball more than Reggie Jackson. And few hit them harder. Jackson, a very aggressive hitter, was almost unstoppable when he got into a groove. Add to that a flair for drama and a huge ego, and you have one of baseball's most memorable sluggers. He was at his best when the spotlight was on him. Jackson hit a monstrous home run during the 1971 All-Star Game and struck the blow that won the 1973 World Series for the Oakland A's. As a member of the Yankees, Jackson clouted three home runs on three swings in the final game of the 1977 World Series to beat the Dodgers. He finished his career with 563 long balls, and the highest slugging percentage in World Series history.

MIKE SCHMIDT   1972–1989

For many generations, third base had been a position manned by defensive stars. Only a few players—including George Kell, Brooks Robinson, and Ron Santo—played the "hot corner" and also hit like All-Stars. The first long ball *specialist* to man third base was Mike Schmidt of the Philadelphia Phillies, a Gold Glove fielder and an eight-time home run champion. Schmidt was a "guess hitter"—he looked for a certain pitch in a certain situation, and if he guessed right he gave it a ride. Unlike most power hitters, who feast on fastballs, he often was looking for an off-speed pitch, like a curve or slider or changeup. Philadelphia fans, who are famously hard on their stars, often booed Schmidt, because when he guessed wrong he could look pretty bad. He looked *good* 548 times during his 18-year career.

MARK McGWIRE 1986–2001

In 1987 Mark McGwire set a new home run record for rookies with 49. Great things were predicted for the lanky young slugger, but pitchers soon learned how to neutralize his power. He responded by swinging harder, and eventually injured his back. In 1993 and 1994—which should have been his prime seasons—"Big Mac" sat out 250 games and hit a mere 18 home runs. During his time off, McGwire rebuilt his body and remade his "long" swing into a compact explosion of brute strength, ignited by a pair of massive forearms. The long balls came fast and furious after that, including 52 in 1996 and 58 in 1997. In 1998, the 34-year-old McGwire broke Roger Maris's single-season record with 70, and followed that with 65 in 1999. McGwire turned himself into a home run machine, with more round-trippers than singles in a typical year. He finished his career with 583 long balls. Had a bad knee not caused McGwire to retire, there is no telling how many more he might have hit.

SAMMY SOSA 1989–Present

No one who saw skinny 20-year-old Sammy Sosa with the Texas Rangers in 1989 imagined he would become one of history's most powerful sluggers. In fact, few thought he would last long in the majors. Sosa swung as hard as he could at anything near the strike zone, getting *himself* out more often than the pitchers did. But as his body developed, and he became smarter about letting the bad pitches go, the long balls began flying off his bat at a record rate. In 1998, he and Mark McGwire went down to the wire in a thrilling home run duel that saw both break Roger Maris's mark. Sosa finished with 66 that year, and hit 50 or more homers a record-tying four years in a row.

BARRY BONDS

In the 1970s, Bobby Bonds was supposed to be "the next Willie Mays." He was a very good player but not a great one, and the fans always felt that he let them down. His son, Barry, came to the Pirates in 1986 with the same kind of buildup, and for his first five years it appeared he might meet the same fate. In 1992, he discarded his long, looping swing and allowed his quick wrists and strong forearms to do the work with a shorter stroke—much as Hank Aaron had done late in his career. A picky hitter with a sharp eye, Bonds became even more selective at the plate—very much as Ted Williams had been. By combining these two qualities, he averaged 40 homers and 120 walks a season over the next nine years. In 2001, Bonds took his game to another level, and broke Mark McGwire's three-year-old record with 73 home runs.

4 Longest, Shortest, Strangest

BASEBALL'S MOST REMARKABLE HOME RUNS

Who hit history's longest home run? There is no simple answer to this question. The distances from home plate to the outfield fences are easy enough to measure, but once a baseball *clears* those fences, science ends and mythology begins. To determine the length of a long ball, do you measure from where it lands or where it finally comes to rest? If the ball's flight is interrupted by a fan in the stadium, part of the stadium itself, or a building outside the stadium, do you calculate where it *would* have landed? Everyone has a different opinion.

After you settle on the best way to measure a home run, you must then decide which home runs count and which do not. Does this record apply to major league games only? Should it include minor league games? What about exhibition games? Amateur games? Does the playing field matter? Do wind, weather, and altitude change anything? And who can be trusted to measure a home run accurately?

Take the case of Babe Ruth, the game's most celebrated slugger. He belted more than 700 balls out of the park during his career, including many that were measured at over 500 feet. In 1927, the same year he became the first player to hit 60 home runs, Ruth crushed a ball over the right-field roof at Comiskey Park in Chicago. Several sportswriters who were stationed high above the playing field confirmed that Ruth's ball cleared the 52-foot-wide roof and continued down into the street. That ball traveled at least 570 feet, but no one saw exactly where it landed, or bothered to measure the distance from home plate at the time.

The left-handed Babe Ruth poses right-handed in a publicity shot taken after he joined the Yankees.

Many believe Ruth's longest blow came in a 1919 spring training contest against the New York Giants in Tampa, Florida. The game was played on the grassy section inside the city's largest racetrack. The inside rail served as the outfield fence. Ruth, who was a member of the Boston Red Sox at the time, stepped into a pitch by George Smith and took a monstrous cut. Wood met horsehide in exactly the right way, and the ball went soaring over the rail in right field. Ross Youngs, one of baseball's fastest players, turned and ran, but he was still more than 100 feet from the ball when it landed on the track. Afterward, Youngs showed sportswriters where the ball had hit, and the spot at which it had come to a stop. A tape measure was produced and the distance of Ruth's blow was set at 579 feet.

For many years, this was regarded as the game's longest long ball. Does the fact that it occurred in a nonofficial game, on a nonofficial field, and was never officially recorded really matter? That is for the fans to decide. It should be noted that the many witnesses to this event—including ballplayers, sportswriters, and team officials—went to their graves saying Ruth's spring training blast was the longest they had ever seen. And these people saw a lot of baseball over the years.

The longest "official" home run is also a matter of debate. Most believe the record belongs to another great slugger, Mickey Mantle. He produced three famous long balls during his career, and each has its own special place in home run history. In 1953, Mantle drove a pitch delivered by Chuck Stobbs of the Washington Senators over the left–center field fence and completely out of Griffith Stadium. The ball is believed to have traveled 565 feet in the air, but there has always been some doubt as to where it landed in the street outside the ballpark.

In 1960, Mantle walloped a ball over the right-field roof of Briggs Stadium in Detroit. No one was

MICKEY MANTLE'S TITANIC 565 FOOT HOME RUN

HIT RIGHT-HANDED, FIFTH INNING, AGAINST WASHINGTON SENATORS, CHUCK STOBBS PITCHING. GRIFFITH STADIUM, APRIL 17, 1953

A dotted line shows the flight of the long ball belted out of Griffith Stadium by Mickey Mantle in 1953.

sure how and where the ball landed, but a mathematician later estimated the ball could have traveled as far as 643 feet in the air. Mantle's most famous homer came in Yankee Stadium off Pedro Ramos of the Senators in 1963. The ball struck the facade atop the right-field stands, and most people who witnessed the blast said the ball was still rising when its flight was interrupted, although this was probably an optical illusion.

Mark McGwire socks his 500th career home run. His longest long ball was not among them—it was hit during a contest prior to the 1999 All-Star Game.

The longest home run in recent years was hit by Mark McGwire during the Home Run Derby at the 1999 All-Star Game in Boston. He launched several bombs completely out of Fenway Park, including one that landed in the street at a distance estimated to be 590 feet from home plate. The longest Home Run Derby blast that has been officially measured was the 524-foot shot by

Sammy Sosa in 2002 at Milwaukee's Miller Park. The longest home run hit *during* an All-Star Game came off the bat of Oakland A's outfielder Reggie Jackson in the 1971 contest at Tiger Stadium. Jackson's ball easily cleared the right-field roof before clanking against the light tower that rose above it. This long ball traveled more than 520 feet before it ricocheted back onto the playing field.

Jose, Can You See?

Sometimes batters need help from the other team to get the ball over the fence. Jose Canseco, who blasted 462 long balls in his career, added a home run to Carlos Martinez's career total (of 25) when a fly ball bounced right off his head and over the fence in a 1993 game.

The record for the longest home run in history—measured from home plate to the spot where it actually came to rest—does not belong to a famous slugger, but to a long-forgotten minor leaguer named Gil Carter. Carter was an outfielder for Carlsbad who led the Class-D Sophomore League with 34 homers in 1959. Number 28 sailed high over a light tower and disappeared into the night. When fans went to retrieve the ball, they found it next to a house some 730 feet away.

Actually, if you measure home runs strictly from the spot they come to a stop, then the record for the longest long ball should go to Charlie "Chief" Zimmer. During the 1890s, Zimmer gained fame as Cy Young's catcher. Zimmer's record-setter was hit out of League Park in Boston against the Red Stockings. Running behind the outfield fence were train tracks, and as luck would have it, a freight train was chugging by at the time. Zimmer's blast landed in an open coal car, and kept going all the way to Fall River, Massachusetts—50 miles away!

Another unusual home run belongs to Andy Oyler, a shortstop who split the 1902 season between the Minneapolis Millers of the American Association and the Baltimore Orioles of the American League. Nicknamed "Pepper" for his feisty, heads-up attitude, Oyler was wearing a Minneapolis uniform when he came to bat in a game against St. Paul. Oyler ducked away from a pitch headed straight for his head, but the ball struck his bat—and ricocheted straight down. Torrential rains had soaked the field the night before, and the ball disappeared into the mud 2 feet in front of home plate. Oyler was the only man in the park who knew where the ball was. He started running—to first, then to second, and then to third—while the St. Paul players searched in vain for the baseball. When Oyler realized they had not yet located it, he sprinted to the plate wearing an ear-to-ear grin. He showed the umpire where the ball was, and was credited with a home run. If the details of this story are accurate, Oyler would be the proud owner of history's *shortest* home run!

Inside Information

Ty Cobb, who retired with history's highest lifetime batting average, specialized in home runs that stayed *in* the park. Although none of his nine homers in 1909 was as short as Andy Oyler's, not a single one of Cobb's "long balls" made it into the stands, either. That year he became the first and only player to lead the league in homers *without* hitting one over the fence.

COBB DETROIT

JACK McINNIS
1st B.—Phil. Athletics
115

Who hit the *sneakiest* home run in history? That honor goes to Jack "Stuffy" McInnis, the star first baseman of the Philadelphia Athletics. In 1911, AL president Ban Johnson decided the best way to speed up games was to limit the number of warm-up tosses pitchers could throw between innings. The rule stated that a new inning would start as soon as the first hitter stepped into the batter's box. No one paid any attention to this rule except McInnis. In a game against the Red Sox, he noticed that the Boston fielders were strolling slowly to their positions while Ed Karger was loosening up on the mound. As Karger lobbed his second practice throw in, McInnis jumped into the batter's box and lofted a ball to the outfield. Under normal circumstances, this would have been an easy catch for center fielder Tris Speaker, but he had just started walking across the infield grass. By the time Speaker realized what had happened and retrieved the ball, McInnis was crossing home plate. After hearing this story, Johnson lifted his ban on warm-up pitches.

SPEAKER-BOSTON-AMER

Fabulous Feats

AN INSIDE LOOK AT THE LONG BALL

The long ball has a life of its own in the legend and lore of baseball. Regardless of whether an unforgettable home run story unfolds in front of millions on national television, or in an obscure minor league ballpark in a faraway time and place, it always seems to find a special spot in history. You do not have to be a great hitter to hit a great home run. The fact is, you can be a lousy one. The trick is to do something no one else has ever done before—and make sure it finds its way into the record books.

Take Jay Clarke, for example. He was a so-so catcher who hit a grand total of six home runs in nine major league seasons. As a 19-year-old minor leaguer, however, Clarke put on history's greatest homer-hitting display. In 1902, his Corsicana club was the terror of the Texas League, winning 27 straight games during one stretch. One of those victories was a 51–3 wipeout of Texarkana. The son of the Texarkana owner was on the mound, and the

J. J. CLARKE, CLEVELAND

Barry (left) and Bobby Bonds make up history's greatest father-son long ball team.

game had been moved to a weird little field with a left-field wall that was no more than 200 feet from home plate. Clarke kept popping balls over the fence, and when the day was done, he had eight home runs—the most ever in a professional game.

The Texas League was also the scene of baseball's only three-homer inning by a player. Gene Rye of the Waco club accomplished this feat in a 1930 game. Another amazing long ball story from the Southwest took place in 1958, when each of the nine starting players for the Douglas Copper Kings homered against the Chihuahua Dorados in a 22–8 win. And before Barry Bonds set baseball's all-time mark for home runs in a season with 73 in 2001, the record was held by Joe Bauman, who blasted 72 for Artesia of the Longhorn League in 1954.

Bonds happens to be one half of history's greatest father-son long ball team. When he hit his 11th round-tripper of the 1987 season, he and his father Bobby surpassed Yogi and Dale Berra's 348 combined home runs. Their total now stands at more than 1,000! If Barry's son ever makes it to the major leagues, the Bonds family will also set a new record for the most homers hit by a father, son, and grandson. As of 2004, that mark belonged to Ray (151), Bob (105), and Bret (245)

Long Ball Brothers

Looks can be deceiving. When two or more baseball brothers combine for a lot of home runs, it is often (but not always) one brother carrying the load.

The Aaron Brothers . . . . .Hank (755) + Tommie (13) = 768
The Alou Brothers . . . . .Felipe (206) + Jesus (32) + Matty (31) = 269
The Boone Brothers . . . . .Bret (245) + Aaron (92) = 337*
The Boyer Brothers . . . . .Ken (282) + Clete (162) + Cloyd (0) = 444
The Brett Brothers . . . . .George (317) + Ken (20) = 337
The Canseco Brothers . . . . .Jose (462) + Ozzie (0) = 462
The DiMaggio Brothers . . . . .Joe (361) + Vince (125) + Dom (87) = 573
The May Brothers . . . . .Lee (354) + Carlos (90) = 444
The Murray Brothers . . . . .Eddie (504) + Rich (4) = 508
The Nettles Brothers .Graig (390) + Jim (16) = 406
The Ripken Brothers . . . . .Cal (431) + Billy (20) = 451

Still playing

Dom (left) and Joe DiMaggio chat before a game at Yankee Stadium. Along with brother Vince, they accounted for 573 home runs.

Boone at 501 (and counting). The most memorable home run by a Boone, however, belongs to Bret's brother, Aaron. He hit an extra-inning long ball in Game 7 of the 2003 American League Championship Series to win the pennant for the New York Yankees.

Bret and Aaron Boone are unusual among baseball brothers because each hits with good power. Hank and Tommie Aaron share the all-time record for home runs by siblings with 768, but Hank accounted for 755 by himself. The same is true for many baseball brothers (see above). Two brothers who knew how to share the long ball spotlight were Ken and Clete Boyer, who combined for 444 home runs. They turned Game 7 of the 1964 World Series into their own personal sibling rivalry when Ken homered for the Cardinals in the seventh inning and Clete went deep for the Yankees in the ninth.

The youngest major leaguer to hit a home run was shortstop Tommy Brown of the Brooklyn Dodgers. With World War II raging and its best players fighting overseas, the club filled out its 1944 roster with several old-timers and a handful of teenagers. Brown was a 16-year-old high schooler when manager Leo Durocher put him into the lineup, and he played 46 games that year, though without hitting a home run. The following year, Brown hit two as a 17-year-old. The oldest major leaguer to go deep? His name was Jack Quinn, and he was a pitcher. Quinn was 47 when he cleared the fence for the A's in 1930.

Rick Ferrell (left) talks baseball with his brother, Wes. Rick holds the career record for home runs by a pitcher, with 37.

Although pitchers are more likely to surrender long balls than hit them these days, there have been many power-hitting hurlers over the years. The greatest, of course, was Babe Ruth, who was so good he was converted to an everyday player. Among the best hitters who stuck to pitching were Wes Ferrell, Warren Spahn, Don Newcombe, and Don Drysdale. Ferrell holds the record among pitchers with 37 career home runs, and the single-season mark with 9. Spahn, who won 373 games, is credited with 35 career long balls, which is the NL record. Newcombe and Drysdale—Dodger teammates in the 1950s—share the NL record of 7 in a season with Mike Hampton, who blasted 7 for the Colorado Rockies in 2001.

Finally, no story about long ball legends would be complete without a few words about the teams and players who made headlines for *not* hitting home runs. Back in the days before the long ball was in style, it was not unusual for a team to finish the year with fewer than 20 home runs, even if it had a good hitter or two. The 1906 Chicago White Sox, who were nicknamed the "Hit-

Life Begins at 75

Hall of Famer Luke Appling was nicknamed "Old Aches and Pains" during his career because he was famous for complaining about every bump and bruise. By 1982—32 years after retiring from baseball—he had recovered enough to put on a uniform for the Old Timer's Classic in Washington, D.C., and take the field. The 75-year-old Appling, who hit just 45 home runs during his 20 years with the Chicago White Sox, stepped up to the plate and drilled a long home run down the left-field line as the crowd watched in open-mouthed awe. There is no official record for the "most surprising" long ball, but it is hard to imagine one more amazing than Appling's.

Sincerely yours
Luke Appling

less Wonders," managed only six home runs all season, but still won the world championship. Two years later, they were almost the "homerless" wonders, with three—the fewest ever. This club may not have been history's weakest, however. By the 1940s, everyone was swinging for the fences—except the Washington Senators. The 1945 team failed to hit a single ball over the fence in their own home park.

The record for the most at bats in a season by a player with no home runs is 672. Rabbit Maranville set the mark with the Pittsburgh Pirates in 1922. While the long ball may be important, he showed that it is not crucial to the success of a player or his team. Maranville was the lead-off hitter for a club that led the league in runs scored that year, and he ended up in the Hall of Fame when he retired.

Nice Grab!

Sometimes the people who catch a famous long ball become famous themselves. Sal Durante, who grabbed Roger Maris's 61st home run in 1961, was a national celebrity. Relief pitcher Tom House became a part of history in 1974 when he caught Hank Aaron's 715th home run. Jeffrey Maier (center, with glove) became the most popular boy in the Bronx—and the most despised in Baltimore—when he reached out over the right-field wall at Yankee Stadium and hauled in a long fly ball hit by Derek Jeter during the 1996 playoffs. The umpires declared it a home run, although replays later showed Maier had actually interfered with outfielder Tony Tarasco. In a weird twist of fate, the two would meet six years later. Maier, by then a high-school baseball player, was attending a clinic featuring—who else?—Tony Tarasco!

Many players have gone an entire career without hitting a home run, but none had more chances than Tom Oliver, who played for the Red Sox in the 1930s. He came to the plate more than 2,000 times and never circled the bases. Tommy Thevenow, an infielder during the same era, went the longest without a true long ball. In 1926, he hit the only two home runs of his 14-year career, and both were inside the park. In the World Series that fall, he was credited with another inside-the-park home run when his hit was misplayed by none other than Babe Ruth.

6 For the Record

BASEBALL'S GREATEST HOME RUN MARKS

Every time a slugger pulls on his uniform, he has a chance to shatter one of baseball's home run marks. Every week, every month, every year he is in the majors, he has the opportunity to etch his name into the record books. The truly historic numbers, however, are reserved for an elite group of sluggers. Yes, records are made to be broken. However, when you have broken one of *these*, you have really done something!

Most in a Season

73—BARRY BONDS, 2001

This record is the one every slugger is shooting for. It takes tremendous power and consistency to hit more than 50 home runs in a season. Imagine trying to hit more than 70!

Most in a Career

755—HANK AARON (RIGHT)

The key to building great career home run totals is learning to adjust your hitting style as you get older. Most players lose their power as they hit their mid-30s, but an elite few are able to keep going and going.

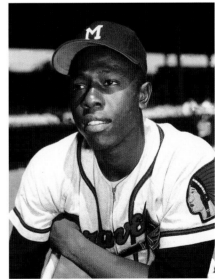

Hank Aaron

Most Years Leading the League

12 — Babe Ruth

It is difficult to compare players from different eras, but you can always tell how good a slugger was compared to his peers by how many times he led the league in long balls.

Most in a Game

4 — By 15 Players
(First: Bobby Lowe, 1894; Last: Carlos Delgado, 2003)

Hitting two home runs in a game is a tremendous accomplishment. Hitting *four* is one of the rarest feats in baseball.

Most 3-Homer Games

6 — Johnny Mize and Sammy Sosa

Most hitters go their entire careers without *one* three-homer game. These stars did it six times each!

Most 2-Homer Games

72 — Babe Ruth

Many of Ruth's records have been broken, but this remains one of his most amazing.

Most by a Rookie

49 — Mark McGwire, 1987

It is not unusual for a young slugger to get off to a fast start in his first year, but major league pitchers usually find a way to cool him off. Despite being unfamiliar with enemy hurlers, McGwire started hot and stayed hot all season long.

Most in a Month

20 — Sammy Sosa, June 1998

Every so often, a hitter gets "locked in" for a week or two—everything he hits seems to rocket off his bat. Sosa found a way to keep it going for an entire month.

Most in a Week

10 — Frank Howard, 1968 (right)

You have to wonder, after six or seven long balls, why pitchers would have thrown Howard a strike the rest of the week.

The 500 Club*

Hank Aaron	755
Babe Ruth	714
Barry Bonds**	703
Willie Mays	660
Frank Robinson	586
Mark McGwire	583
Sammy Sosa**	574
Harmon Killebrew	573
Reggie Jackson	563
Rafael Palmeiro**	551
Mike Schmidt	548
Mickey Mantle	536
Jimmie Foxx	534
Ted Williams	521
Willie McCovey	521
Eddie Mathews	512
Ernie Banks	512
Mel Ott	511
Eddie Murray	504
Ken Griffey Jr.**	501

* Through the 2004 season
** Active in 2005

Frank Howard

Most by a Team

264—SEATTLE MARINERS, 1997

Home runs are nice, but they do not always win ball games. The 1997 Mariners hit 264 long balls and won 90 games, while the 2001 Mariners hit only 169 homers but won 116.

Most in a World Series Game

3—BABE RUTH AND REGGIE JACKSON

Baseball's biggest showmen had their greatest games on baseball's biggest stage.

Most World Series Home Runs in a Career

18—MICKEY MANTLE

Mantle loved playing for the championship. He averaged one long ball every 15.1 at bats during the regular season, but one every 12.7 at bats during the World Series.

Most All-Star Home Runs

6—STAN MUSIAL

There are no second-rate pitchers on the mound during All-Star competition—"Stan the Man" hit every one of his long balls off a top hurler.

Most Consecutive Games with a Home Run

8—DALE LONG, DON MATTINGLY, AND KEN GRIFFEY JR.

This is one of baseball's most exciting—and remarkable—records.

Most Grand Slams in a Season

6—DON MATTINGLY (RIGHT)

Subtract the six grand slams Mattingly hit in 1987, and a great season would have looked very ordinary: 24 home runs and 91 RBIs instead of 30 home runs and 115 RBIs.

Most Grand Slams in a Career

23—LOU GEHRIG

Gehrig batted after either Babe Ruth or Joe DiMaggio most of his career. Pitchers often decided to walk these stars and take their chances with Gehrig, even if it meant loading the bases. Obviously, he took it personally!

The 60 Home Run Club*

73	Barry Bonds, 2001
70	Mark McGwire, 1998
66	Sammy Sosa, 1998
65	Mark McGwire, 1999
64	Sammy Sosa, 2001
63	Sammy Sosa, 1999
61	Roger Maris, 1961
60	Babe Ruth, 1927

Through the 2004 season

Don Mattingly

7 Baseball's Greatest Hit

THE FUTURE OF THE HOME RUN

Whenever baseball has been in trouble, it has turned to the long ball. Home runs draw crowds to the ballpark, increase the sport's television ratings, and keep fans excited about teams long after they have faded from the pennant race. Even in times of war, economic struggle, and scandal, the home run has boosted the fortunes of the game. But what happens when the long ball *itself* is in trouble—what is baseball to do when every slugger is a target of suspicion, and every home run is called into question?

Baseball has had to face this dilemma in recent years. During the 1980s and 1990s, there were whispers around major league locker rooms that some players were using "performance-enhancing" drugs to gain an edge over the competition. These included products that could be bought at health food stores, such as androstenedione (which is now banned), as well as substances that were illegal unless prescribed by a doctor, including human growth hormone and anabolic steroids.

When a handful of retired stars admitted they had used steroids and other drugs during their playing days, fans became very angry.

In his book *Juiced!*, Jose Canseco—the first player to hit 40 homers and steal 40 bases in the same year—wrote that he used steroids to help him build the muscles he needed to succeed. Although Canseco had no way of proving it, he also claimed that many players in the game had done the same. This cast grave doubts on the home run records set by Mark McGwire, Sammy Sosa, Barry Bonds, and others.

Jose Canseco is sworn in at the 2005 congressional hearings on steroid use in baseball. Canseco admitted using steroids and accused many others of doing the same.

In 2005, Congress held a special hearing to investigate the steroid problem in baseball. Several players and executives, including commissioner Bud Selig, testified that day. Selig explained that the sport's "hands were tied" because of a complicated agreement with the union that represented the players. Baseball was not allowed to test most players for steroids; those who were tested and caught received very light punishment. The politicians on the panel

What *Are* Steroids?

There are many types of steroids and other "performance-enhancing" substances, all of which are banned by baseball. Not a single one is meant to be used by athletes. Taking them without a prescription is against the law.

Steroids do not "grow" muscles as some fans believe. Athletes who take illegal steroids recover quickly from strenuous workouts, which means less rest time *between* workouts—which develops muscles faster. Unfortunately, the same process that appears to build *up* the body is actually breaking it *down*. Steroid abuse has led to many muscle injuries, and actually shortened the careers of many players.

became very angry. They felt that the game was not being honest with the fans. They also believed that steroid use in baseball had led to many deaths among young people who thought it was okay to take them—and would lead to

Please Say No!

The long-term effects of steroid use are not fully known, but what *is* known is not good—athletes like Jose Canseco are likely to develop a number of life-threatening conditions, and many will die young. Ken Caminiti, the 1996 National League MVP, admitted to using steroids that year. He did not enjoy this accomplishment very long. In 2004, he suffered a massive heart attack and died at the age of 40. As terrible a loss as this was, the bigger tragedy is that, for every famous athlete who pays the ultimate price for steroid abuse, hundreds more will soon suffer the same fate. And they won't be famous. They'll just be dead.

many, many more. It was a dark day for the game.

Among the many who raised their voices in anger was Mike Greenwell. Greenwell was an All-Star outfielder for the Boston Red Sox whose career ended in 1996. He finished runner-up to Jose Canseco for the Most Valuable Player Award in 1988. Greenwell wondered why the MVP should be sitting in Canseco's trophy case and not his. Canseco admitted breaking the rules and gaining an unfair advantage. Should he not forfeit the MVP? In track and field and other sports, Greenwell pointed out, cheaters can have their awards taken away and their records erased. Why not do the same in baseball?

Baseball has always been reluctant to tinker with its records. The sport's statistics are all linked to one another like a big math equation, so changing one number would mean changing thousands. Even the records of players who were caught losing games on purpose are still counted. But what about taking away an MVP award? Or a home run championship? Like it or not, these awards are linked to statistics, too. So it is unlikely that baseball will use its awards as a means of punishing players who break the rules.

Where baseball *does* have the power to go back and "punish" cheaters is when players become eligible for the Hall of Fame. Some of the game's greatest players were blocked from Cooperstown because they broke baseball's rules, including Joe Jackson (a .356 lifetime hitter) and Pete Rose (the all-time hit king with 4,256). If it is proven that today's sluggers used steroids to boost their long ball totals, it will be interesting to see how the Hall of Fame voters treat them after they retire.

If a player admits to using steroids, will he also be banned from the Hall of Fame? Not necessarily. Don't forget, it is incredibly difficult to hit a home run off of a major league pitcher. There is no pill or shot or cream you can use to hit a home run. Steroids might speed up a player's swing by a tiny percentage—and that tiny percentage may make the difference between a long out and a long ball a couple of times a season—but only the best players can connect with that pitch in the first place.

Although the future may be unclear for some of the game's best long ball hitters, the long ball itself seems to be safe. Hitters are getting stronger, ballparks are getting smaller, and the fans still love to see home runs. History is a very good teacher, and in this case it tells us not to worry. The long ball will *always* be baseball's greatest hit.

Joe Carter cannot contain his joy after hitting the home run that ended the 1993 World Series. Moments like this make the long ball baseball's "greatest hit."

Index

Page numbers in italics refer to illustrations.